COIN COLLECTING

BOY SCOUTS OF AMERICA
IRVING, TEXAS

Requirements

1. Understand how coins are made, and where the active U.S. Mint facilities are located.

2. Explain these collecting terms:

   a. Obverse

   b. Reverse

   c. Reeding

   d. Clad

   e. Type set

   f. Date set

3. Explain the grading terms poor, good, very good, fine, very fine, extremely fine, and uncirculated. Show five different grade examples of the same coin type. Explain the term "proof" and why it is not a grade. Tell what "encapsulated" coins are.

4. Know three different ways to store a collection, and describe the benefits, drawbacks, and expense of each method. Pick one to use when completing requirements.

5. Do the following:

   a. Demonstrate to your counselor that you know how to use two U.S. or world coin reference catalogs.

   b. Read a numismatic magazine or newspaper and tell your counselor about what you learned.

6. Describe the 1999–2008 50 State Quarters program. Collect and show your counselor five different state quarters you have acquired from circulation.

7. Collect from circulation a set of current U.S. coins. Include one coin of each denomination (cent, nickel, dime, quarter, half dollar, dollar). For each coin, locate the mint marks, if any, and the designer's initials, if any.

8. Do the following:

   a. Identify the people depicted on the following denominations of current U.S. paper money: $1, $2, $5, $10, $20, $50, and $100.

   b. Explain "legal tender."

   c. Describe the role the Federal Reserve System plays in the distribution of currency.

9. Do ONE of the following:

   a. Collect and identify 50 foreign coins from at least 10 different countries.

   b. Collect and identify 20 bank notes from at least five different countries.

   c. Collect and identify 15 different tokens or medals.

   d. Collect a date set of a single type since the year of your birth.

10. Do ONE of the following:

   a. Tour a U.S. Mint facility, a Bureau of Engraving and Printing facility, or a Federal Reserve bank, and describe what you learned to your counselor.

   b. With your parent's permission, attend a coin show or coin club meeting, or view the Web site of the U.S. Mint or a coin dealer, and report what you learned.

   c. Give a talk about coin collecting to your troop or class at school.

   d. Do drawings of five Colonial-era U.S. coins.

33390A
ISBN 978-0-8395-3390-0
©2002 Boy Scouts of America
2007 Printing

Contents

Introduction

Coin collecting is one of the oldest of all hobbies. Hoards of ancient coins found in excavations indicate that coins were one of the first collectibles. From earliest times, people valued coins not only as a means of trading and storing wealth, but also as miniature works of art. As early as the 15th century, coin collectors began keeping coins for historical significance and not just for their monetary value.

When you hold an old coin in your hand, you make a connection with people, places, and events of another time. Imagine who first used that coin, how many times it changed hands, and where the coin traveled. Owning a coin is like owning a piece of history.

Coins are universal and timeless. Every piece is worthy of being saved. People recognize coinage—no matter how odd or foreign. By preserving the past, collectors create a legacy for the future.

Happily, you do not have to spend a lot of money to enjoy collecting coins. Thousands of coins are available for less than $1 each. Some pieces from the Roman Empire may be acquired for as little as $5. On the other hand, collecting can become an extreme challenge, with collectors bidding against one another at auctions in attempts to own rare or exotic pieces.

Coin collectors enjoy the thrill of acquiring prized pieces, assembling a fine collection, and even selling some of their coins for a profit. But they also value learning about the various forms of *currency* as well as sharing a common interest with other collectors. It is no wonder that more than 3 million Americans participate in coin collecting in one form or another!

Coin collecting, so long the hobby of kings, is truly the king of hobbies.

Numismatics

nu–miz–mat´–iks

The study or collection of coins, medals, tokens, and paper money.

A Treasury of Coin Terms

In this pamphlet, the first mention of these terms is shown in italics.

You will encounter the following terms as you learn about the hobby of coin collecting.

alloy. A combination of two or more metals.

back. The backside of a piece of paper money, opposite the face.

bank note. A piece of paper money issued by a banking institution.

cast. To manufacture coins by pouring molten metal into a one- or two-piece mold.

circulation. Passage of coins, notes, and bills currently in use as money from person to person.

commemorative. A special coin issued to mark an event or honor a person or place.

currency. All coins and paper money in circulation.

date set. A collection of coins of a single type and denomination, including every date since a particular year; for example, the Lincoln cent from 1988 to the present.

decoration. An award presented to an individual by a government authority for service to a country; the decoration is meant to be worn.

denomination. The face value of a coin or paper note.

designer's initials. The initials of the artist who created the coin's design; usually two or three very small letters found on or near the design.

die. A metal block engraved with a design in reverse for use in striking coins.

die crack. An irregular raised line on the surface of a struck coin, caused by the coin metal pushing through a crack in the die.

edge. The vertical side of a coin, often called the third side, with a smooth, lettered, or security-enhanced surface such as reeding.

error. A coin or bank note on which a mistake was made during its production.

face. The front of a piece of paper money, often with a portrait.

field. The smooth area of a coin's surface where there is no design or legend.

grades. Rating terms collectors use to describe the level of wear on a coin.

inscription. The words or letters that run across the field of a coin or medal.

legal tender. Coins or paper money issued by a government that is accepted as a valid form of payment.

legend. The words or letters that circle the inside border of a side of a coin or medal.

medal. A large round metal object struck as an award or commemoration; it is not legal tender and is meant to be displayed, not worn.

mintage. The number of coins actually struck during one minting period.

mint mark. A symbol or letter used to indicate which mint struck the coin.

mule. A coin, token, or medal struck from two dies not meant to be paired together.

obverse. The front (or "heads") side of a coin; usually bears the more important legends, portraits, or design elements.

paper money. The general term given to bank notes, scrip, and other paper items used as currency.

planchet. The blank metal disk on which a coin design is struck.

reeding. The grooved vertical lines around the edge of a coin.

relief. The part of a coin's design that is raised above the surface.

reverse. The back (or "tails") side of a coin; usually bears the design of lesser importance and may feature a commemorative event.

series. A set of coins of a particular design including one example of each year, from each mint; for example, Jefferson nickels, 1939 to the present.

slab. A coin that has been encapsulated in a plastic holder by a professional grading or authentication service.

strike. The process of stamping a coin, token, or medal; involves pressing obverse and reverse dies together on a planchet with great force.

token. A coinlike object issued by a company or private firm for use in transactions; it is not legal tender.

type. A general term for a coin's distinguishing design, such as the Roosevelt dime.

type set. A set of coins of a particular denomination that includes all the designs; can be expanded to include other denominations and designs, such as a 20th century type set.

watermark. An impression left in paper during the manufacturing process, which is visible when the paper is held up to the light; used to deter counterfeiting.

A steam-powered coining press, used at the Paris Mint in the 1860s

Coins in the Making

Whether you are collecting irregular shaped ancient gold coins or the 50 State Quarters, you will be a more knowledgeable collector if you have a general understanding of how coins are made.

People *cast* early coins by pouring molten metal into molds that were engraved with designs. People also engraved designs into anvils to create *dies*. The coin maker would place a lump of metal on the anvil and then *strike* it with a hammer to force the metal into the design. Later the Romans used hinged dies, which allowed a heated hand-cut *planchet* to receive designs on both sides.

The U.S. Mint shipped about 12.5 billion coins in 2003. Surely some of them have found their way into your pockets.

Early Machine-Struck Coins

As trade developed throughout Europe, the need to accelerate the minting process and to standardize the appearance of *currency* led to machine-struck coins. The strong and even pressure of the screw (or mill) press, invented in the mid-1500s, created coins with uniform shapes and sharper images.

The screw press required several people to operate it. It produced uniform coins, but at a slow pace.

On the roller press, invented in the 16th century, a strip of metal passed between two cylinders that had multiple designs engraved on them. The cylinders impressed *obverse* and *reverse* designs on the sheet, which was then cut into many coins.

Counterfeiting became such a serious problem during the Renaissance period (14th through 16th centuries) that people caught doing it were often executed. Some criminals trimmed the *edges* of gold and silver coins to steal the metal. To prevent

A screw press, used at the Paris Mint in the 1780s

these activities, coiners fitted a collar, or retaining ring, around each planchet and then struck the blank. This formed a perfectly round, smooth-edged coin. Eventually, the collar was treated like a third die, with a *legend* or design engraved on the inside surface. After about 1800, the edge marks often were grooved vertical lines called *reeding*, like those on the edges of today's quarters.

Mass-Produced Coins

In the 1790s in Birmingham, England, Matthew Boulton and James Watt developed the steam-powered coin press. Unlike the screw press, which required several operators and was slow, the steam press struck the planchet with a solid stroke. This produced coins of uniform size and design with great speed and accuracy—and the press required only one operator.

The reducing machine was another invention that increased the production of coins. It made an actual-size tracing of a coin design from a large-scale model of the design. From this tracing, or hub, the master die and working dies were made. Early dies were cut by hand; the hub allowed many identical dies to be made.

Today's dies last a long time because they are made of specially hardened steel.

Coin Making the Modern Way

The U.S. Mint buys strips of metal that are the thickness of a coin and measure about 13 inches wide and more than 1,500 feet long. The strips are wound into coils and fed through a blanking press, which punches out disks, called coin blanks.

After going through the blanking press, the strips, now punched full of holes, are called webbing and get shredded and recycled into more strips.

Next, the blanks are heated in a furnace to soften them. Then they are run through a washer and dryer to remove any grease. A machine called a riddler sorts the shiny blanks to screen out irregular ones.

An upsetting mill squeezes the edges, giving the blanks a slightly raised rim. This allows the coins to be stacked. When the blanks are placed into the coining press, dies strike the designs and legends. This stamping makes the blanks real U.S. coins.

Various people and machines inspect, count, and bag the new coins for shipment to Federal Reserve banks, which distribute them to local banks.

Special Coins

Certain coins are never meant for *circulation*. Some are specially minted for sale to collectors; others are prepared to test designs during the production process. These special coins are produced in small quantities.

Essay. The essay coin is a new, changed, or proposed coin design, often with "ESSAI" stamped in the *field*.

Pattern. A pattern is a proposed coin of new design, denomination, or metal, that is not adopted during the year it is struck.

Proof. A proof coin is the highest quality coin because the utmost care is taken during the minting process to produce a flawless coin. The mint polishes the dies and metal blanks before striking. Sometimes the dies are sandblasted to create "frosted" features that contrast with the polished surfaces of the field. Proof coins can be distinguished by their sharp detail, brilliant mirrorlike surface, and sharp rims. The term "proof" describes the way the coin was made and should not be confused with a *grade*.

Specimen. A specimen is a coin of regular design and metal that is made for presentation. It is struck at greater than normal pressure with specially prepared dies and planchets.

Trial strike. A trial strike is a test piece, often of an incomplete design, made during die preparation. It usually is struck with a single die. Because the trial strike is never meant to leave the mint, it is a rare find.

Clad Coinage

In the 1960s, many countries stopped using silver in their circulating coins because the metal content was worth more than the face value. (There was more than 25 cents' worth of silver in a quarter!) Rather than creating coins with new designs to replace silver coins, such as the dime and quarter, the U.S. Mint stamped the standard designs on coins made of several layers of different metals. These sandwich coins are called clad coinage. Typical clad coins have a copper core surrounded by layers of copper-nickel *alloy* that make the coins look silver.

Coins Through the Ages

Before people used coins in exchange for goods, they traded with hand-fashioned gold and silver pieces called ingots. These varied in size and shape as well as in value. At every transaction, the merchant or trader had to weigh each ingot and verify that the metal was genuine. Later, ingots were stamped with a seal that described the weight, contents, and purity of the metal. People realized that it was much easier to do business with stamped ingots.

In Greek and Roman times, coins were a way to spread news, propaganda, and ideas because the coins circulated widely to all classes of people for long periods of time.

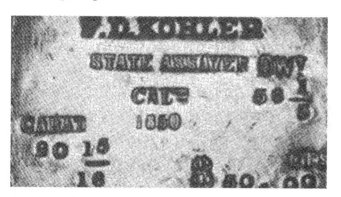

Gold ingot, circa mid-1800s

Ancient Coins

Coins were made in the Mediterranean, Central Asian, and Far East regions between 650 and 600 B.C. The most famous of these first coins are from the Greek kingdom of Lydia (located in modern-day western Turkey). They are made of electrum (a natural alloy of gold and silver) and carry a stamped lion's head on the obverse and crude markings on the reverse.

Lydian stater featuring the foreparts of a lion and a bull, 600 B.C.

Traders used early coins because they offered an easy way to tote precious metals.

Coins made of electrum did not always contain equal portions of gold and silver, so the value among coins differed even if the weights were equal. Eventually, metal refining improved, and the Greeks started making nearly pure gold or silver coins in *denominations,* such as the stater and tetradrachm.

With the decline of Greek power, coins of the Roman Empire (30 B.C. to A.D. 425) replaced Greek coins in the Mediterranean region. Roman coins often have the emperor's portrait or those of his family members on the obverse. The design on the reverse features a temple, shrine, or monument of which the local inhabitants were particularly proud. The coins, in denominations such as the gold aureus, silver denarius, and bronze sestertius, are important because they are the only visual records left of buildings long gone.

People on the Indian subcontinent also created marked metal coins. The thick Indian coins often included only *inscriptions.*

The Chinese developed cast copper coins with distinctive square holes in the center. The coins, called "cash," could be strung together and carried around. Except for changes in the legends to identify the ruler, denomination, and mint, early designs were unchanged until replaced by machine-struck coins in the 1870s.

Medieval Coins

When the Western Roman Empire fell into chaos in the fifth century, the Byzantines shut down many of the Roman mints and opened their own.

During the Golden Age in the fourth and third centuries B.C., the Greeks created some of the most beautiful coins ever minted. The coins, stamped on thick planchets with high-*relief* designs, feature portraits of gods and goddesses or political emblems on the obverse, and mythical animals or individual civic badges on the reverse. *Mint marks* identify which cities minted the coins.

Tetradrachm, with Alexander the Great on the obverse and Zeus on the reverse

Tetradrachm, with Athena on the obverse and owl on the reverse

Byzantine minters followed Roman coin-making traditions but introduced new features, such as Christian symbols. They later replaced Latin inscriptions with Greek letters.

Until the 11th century, minters struck coins on flat planchets. As centuries passed, the quality of the artistry and engraving on the Byzantine coins deteriorated.

During the fifth and sixth centuries, the Islamic world expanded. The Arab conquerors had no coinage of their own, so they issued coins that imitated Byzantine coins. However, the new coins featured only inscriptions, such as the names of rulers or quotations from the Koran, the sacred scriptures of Islam.

Medieval coins of Europe were very thin with legends written in Latin, a cross on the reverse, and portraits rendered in very basic form—quite a change from the realistic depictions on Greek and Roman coins.

The discovery of silver deposits in Joachimsthal in Bohemia led to the production of large silver coins nicknamed Joachimsthalers. The name was shortened to thaler or taler, eventually becoming the dollar.

As trade expanded, countries made coins that featured national themes. In the early 1500s, realistic depictions of rulers reappeared on coin designs. Currencies from France, England, and Italy became widely known along trade routes, and were accepted and imitated in many different areas of the world.

In ancient Greece, the largest silver coins used for small change were no wider than a pencil eraser. Because the ancient Greeks did not have pockets or purses, they carried the coins in their mouths. However, they did not do that with bronze coins, which tasted awful and might have poisoned them!

Coins in the United States

Early settlers traded with American Indians and other colonists, using wampum (strands of beads), animal skins, tobacco, tea, musket balls, and salt as money. As more immigrants and traders arrived in America, the demand for coins increased. Foreign coins of all kinds were accepted, particularly the Spanish "piece of eight," which became the standard money unit throughout the Colonial period.

Two Bits, Four Bits, Eight Bits, A Dollar!

The Spanish milled dollar, or piece of eight, was often cut into pieces to make change. Each piece, or bit, was worth 12^{1}/2 cents. That is why people often call the quarter "two bits."

Colonial-Era Coins

England would not provide small change currency to the Colonies, so certain Colonies and individuals took matters into their own hands. In the Massachusetts Bay Colony, John Hull minted the NE (New England) shilling. The coin was easy to counterfeit, so it was replaced with a *series* of tree coins: the pine, oak, and willow. These tree coins were minted for 30 years, from 1652 to 1682, but almost all bear the date of 1652. This was done so King Charles II of England could not prove the coins had been minted continuously without his approval.

NE (New Englnd) shilling (top) and Pine Tree shilling, obverse sides, 1652

In Maryland, Cecil Calvert (Lord Baltimore) arranged for coins to be minted in England for use in the Colony. Because the English king, Charles I, had recently been beheaded, Calvert was not afraid to put his own portrait on the obverse.

Lord Baltimore shilling, 1659

Once the Declaration of Independence was signed in 1776, a national coinage was proposed. The Continental Dollar was the first pattern coin struck for the United States of America. The obverse carries the Latin legend *FUGIO* (I fly) and the inscription "Mind Your Business." People interpret the message as "Time flies, so mind your business." The reverse design, suggested by Benjamin Franklin, shows 13 linked circles, each with a Colony's name, and the center inscription "We Are One."

Continental Dollar, 1776

State Coins

The Articles of Confederation (1781) established a central government, but gave the states enough power to act almost like separate countries. While statesmen tried to develop a national coinage, certain states minted their own coins. Vermont, New Jersey, and Connecticut contracted with individual silversmiths to make coins; Massachusetts created its own mint.

Vermont cent, 1785, obverse and reverse

New Jersey cent, 1786, obverse and reverse

Connecticut cent, 1787, obverse and reverse

Massachusetts cent, 1787, obverse and reverse

National Coins

Once the Constitution was ratified and a strong central govern-ment was in place, Congress established a national coinage. In 1792, it passed a bill creating the United States Mint in the nation's capital, Philadelphia, Pennsylvania. The bill called for coins to be minted in gold, silver, and copper in 10 denomina-tions as needed.

Coins of the New Nation

Denomination	Value	Year First Struck
Gold Eagle	$ 10.00	1795
Gold Half Eagle	$ 5.00	1795
Gold Quarter Eagle	$ 2.50	1796
Silver Dollar	$ 1.00	1794
Silver Half Dollar	$ .50	1794
Silver Quarter Dollar	$ .25	1796
Silver Disme (dime)	$ .10	1796
Silver Half Disme	$ .05	1794
Copper Cent	$ .01	1793
Copper Half Cent	$ .005	1793

George Washington was so popular that many people wanted his portrait on the new U.S. coins. After all, other countries had for centuries put images of their rulers on coins. But an American president served for four years at a time, not for life like monarchs and emperors. It would be confusing to change coin designs after each election. So the first U.S. coins bear a female representation of liberty.

Expansion of the U.S. Mint

From 1793 to 1838, the U.S. Mint in Philadelphia was the only mint in operation. But when gold was discovered in various areas of the country, the U.S. Mint opened branches in Charlotte, North Carolina; Dahlonega, Georgia; and New Orleans, Louisiana. Later, gold was found in California and gold prices skyrocketed. By 1853, the abundance of gold and the high demand for gold coins prompted the government to open a branch mint in San Francisco, which began operation in 1854.

Why Are Mint Marks Important?

Collectors use mint marks as one way to determine a coin's value. One mint might strike a large quantity of a particular coin, and another might strike a small quantity. The coin produced in smaller quantities is rarer, and therefore more valuable to a collector.

Morgan silver dollar, struck from 1878 to 1904 and in 1921

The U.S. Mint opened another branch in Carson City, Nevada, after the discovery of silver in the Comstock Lode in Nevada. With plenty of silver available, the U.S. Mint introduced a new silver dollar design featuring a Liberty Head on the obverse and an eagle within a wreath on the reverse. Collectors commonly call this the Morgan dollar, based on the name of the designer, George T. Morgan.

To distinguish the branch coins from the Philadelphia coins, the dies carried a mint mark, or letter, in the field to identify which branch made what coins.

Mints and Their Marks

C	Charlotte Mint, North Carolina
CC	Carson City Mint, Nevada
D	Dahlonega Mint, Georgia
D	Denver Mint, Colorado (20th and 21st centuries)
O	New Orleans Mint, Louisiana
P	Philadelphia Mint, Pennsylvania
S	San Francisco Mint, California
W	West Point Mint, New York

Today, four mints are active: Denver, Philadelphia, San Francisco, and West Point.

The 1907 high-relief $20 gold pieces were called experimental and are now considered by many to be not only the most beautiful U.S. coins, but also great rarities.

The Art of the Coin

President Theodore Roosevelt, famous for leading the Rough Riders during the Spanish-American War, also battled for better coin designs. He loved the classical coins of ancient Greece and hired well-known sculptor Augustus Saint-Gaudens to design new gold coins. The first 1907 gold coins had extremely high relief, which pleased Roosevelt but dismayed bankers, who complained that the coins would not stack. The relief was lowered and coins were struck and circulated.

Roosevelt's influence affected copper and silver coin designs, too. In 1909, a portrait of Abraham Lincoln replaced the American Indian portrait on the cent. The Indian Head cent had circulated for 50 years. Later, an American Indian

1907 High Relief Double Eagle by Augustus Saint-Gaudens

portrait with an American bison (buffalo) on the reverse replaced the Liberty Head nickel. In 1916, the U.S. Mint introduced the Winged Liberty (Mercury) dime, Standing Liberty quarter, and Walking Liberty half dollar. The Morgan dollar was replaced by the Peace dollar design in 1922.

1909 Lincoln/Wheat Ears cent, reverse designed by Victor D. Brenner (VDB)

1915 American Indian Head/Buffalo nickel, designed by James E. Fraser (JF)

Prominent sculptors of the day designed the coins, and they received credit by having their initials on the coins bearing their designs.

1916 Winged Liberty (Mercury) dime, designed by Adolph A. Weinman (AAW)

1916 Standing Liberty quarter, designed by Hermon A. MacNeil (M)

1920 Walking Liberty half dollar, designed by Adolph A. Weinman (AAW)

Obverse   Reverse

DESIGN

FIELD

INSCRIPTION

DATE

LEGEND

MINT MARK

DESIGNER'S INITIALS

RIM

DENOMINATION

Parts of a coin, as shown on the 1922 Peace dollar

Some designs come from national competitions. Anthony de Francisci (AF) won the competition for the 1922 Peace dollar, and Felix Schlag (FS) won for the 1938 Jefferson nickel. Participation in those competitions was by invitation. The U.S. Mint sponsored an open competition for the bicentennial of the Declaration of Independence. Nearly a thousand people—from children to professional engravers—submitted designs for the reverses of the quarter, half dollar, and dollar.

Starting in 1932, with the bicentennial of George Washington's birth, circulating silver coins began to honor famous Americans. Though it was intended to be a one-year *commemorative* issue, the Washington quarter was so popular it returned in 1934 to annual production.

In 1946, the U.S. Mint honored Franklin Delano Roosevelt, president through the Great Depression and World War II, by putting his portrait on the dime. Two years later, Benjamin Franklin appeared on the half dollar, with the Liberty Bell on the reverse. This design would have circulated for 25 years, but after President Kennedy was assassinated, the U.S. Mint replaced the Franklin half dollar with the John F. Kennedy design in 1964.

The Dollar Coin Doldrums

The Peace dollar was discontinued in 1935, and no silver dollars were minted until the Eisenhower dollar appeared in 1971. It circulated for eight years before it was replaced by the smaller Susan B. Anthony dollar, which was intended to honor the suffrage movement heroine. But the Susan B. Anthony dollar was poorly conceived. People confused it with the quarter because it had the same color and reeded edge. The public saw no need to use the small dollar coin because the paper dollar was still being made.

Eisenhower dollar, Susan B. Anthony dollar, and Sacagawea dollar

In 2000, the U.S. Mint introduced the Sacagawea dollar, which is sometimes called the Golden dollar although it contains no gold. Congress (which legislates coinage design) and the U.S. Mint changed the design from the Susan B. Anthony dollar. The coin is a distinctive color and has a smooth edge. However, because the paper dollar still circulates, the coin is not widely used. Some vending machines do not even accept it!

United States Commemorative Coins

The 1892–93 Chicago world's fair celebrated the 400th anniversary of Christopher Columbus's exploration of the New World. The organizers of the World's Columbian Exposition won approval from Congress to commemorate the 1892 event with specially designed quarter- and half dollar coins. Today, collectors know these as the Isabella quarter and the Columbian Exposition half dollar.

Isabella quarter issued in 1893 to commemorate the Columbian Exposition. Queen Isabella of Spain is on the obverse.

In 1900, the U.S. Mint featured George Washington and the Marquis de Lafayette on a commemorative silver dollar. Later, commemoratives issued in various denominations, such as the gold $1, $2.50, and $50 coins, honored Lewis and Clark, President William McKinley, President Thomas Jefferson, and the Panama-Pacific Exposition of 1915. Most of the circulating commemoratives from 1912 through 1954 were silver half dollars. Some of the subjects honored include the Battle of Gettysburg, Stone Mountain Memorial (home of the world's largest exposed granite monolith), and such people as George Washington Carver, who was born a slave and became one of this country's most celebrated agriculturalists and educators.

The bicentennial of the Declaration of Independence prompted changes to the reverse of the circulating quarter, half

After 1954, the government halted production of commemorative coins because the process was being overused and abused. Certain groups tried to increase profits by convincing Congress to allow coin production at all the mints, which created three different coins to sell to collectors. Or they convinced Congress to keep *mintages* low, which created rarities.

dollar, and dollar for the years 1975 and 1976. The new design was popular, and commemorative coinage in the United States resumed in 1982 with the commemorative half dollar in honor of the 250th anniversary of George Washington's birth. Recent commemorative coins have honored Mount Rushmore, the Library of Congress, the 1984 and 2002 Olympic Games, the Centennial of the Statue of Liberty, and the Bicentennial of the Constitution.

Congress revived commemoratives in 1982.

Most commemorative coins are legal tender, but are not meant for circulation. The U.S. Mint produces most of these coins in limited quantities for a limited time.

1928 Oregon Trail Memorial silver half dollar

1937 Battle of Antietam 75th anniversary (1862–1937) silver half dollar. Civil War opposing generals Lee and McClellan are pictured on the obverse.

Bullion Coinage

Bullion is nearly pure precious metal, usually in the form of ingots. Although it often refers to gold, bullion also includes silver platinum and palladium.

After the 1929 stock market crash, people hoarded gold. Removing so much gold from circulation seriously affected the stability of the U.S. economy. The Gold Hoarding Act of 1933 made it illegal for citizens to hold gold coins and bullion.

Gradually, the government lifted restrictions and legalized gold ownership in the 1970s. Gold bullion medallions were coined in 1974 and 1975 to honor people in the fine arts, but the medallions did not have denominations, were hard to order, and were unpopular. In the 1980s, the government decided to strike bullion coins in gold, silver, and platinum with denominations.

> Investors buy bullion coins for two reasons: (1) The value of rare bullion coins goes up when the numismatic demand for these coins goes up, and (2) the natural value of bullion coins fluctuates with the price of the metal.

The 50 State Quarters Program

In 1999, the U.S. Mint released the first five quarters in the 50 State Quarters program. This series honors each of the 50 states. The program runs from 1999 through 2008, with five new quarters released every year for 10 years. The new coins share the same obverse depicting George Washington, but have

different designs on the reverse.

Each state is responsible for the design of its quarter. State governors call for design ideas, often through statewide competitions. Then each governor submits five designs to the Mint for renderings. The Commission of Fine Arts and the Citizens Coinage Advisory Committee make recommendations to the Secretary of the U.S. Department of the Treasury, who makes the final selection.

New York, January 2

North Carolina, March 12

Rhode Island, May 21

Vermont, August 6

Kentucky, October 15

The 2001 State Quarters and their release dates

The 50 State Quarters are issued in the order of each state's admission into the Union:

1999   Delaware, Pennsylvania, New Jersey, Georgia, Connecticut

2000   Massachusetts, Maryland, South Carolina, New Hampshire, Virginia

2001   New York, North Carolina, Rhode Island, Vermont, Kentucky

2002   Tennessee, Ohio, Louisiana, Indiana, Mississippi

2003   Illinois, Alabama, Maine, Missouri, Arkansas

2004   Michigan, Florida, Texas, Iowa, Wisconsin

2005   California, Minnesota, Oregon, Kansas, West Virginia

2006   Nevada, Nebraska, Colorado, North Dakota, South Dakota

2007   Montana, Washington, Idaho, Wyoming, Utah

2008   Oklahoma, New Mexico, Arizona, Alaska, Hawaii

Congress may extend the program to include the District of Columbia, Puerto Rico, Guam, American Samoa, U.S. Virgin Islands, and Northern Mariana Islands.

Paper Money

Paper currency like the kind we use today was created in China in the 14th century. The Chinese printed paper money from a large wood-block impression depicting groups of "cash" coins, which were familiar to people as currency.

As the European economy expanded in the 17th century, merchants needed a more convenient way to transport sums of money. Paper documents let the merchants carry the equivalent of large amounts of gold or silver over long distances in hazardous conditions. In time, banks and national governments issued paper notes to represent silver or gold held on deposit, and the public gradually accepted these paper notes in transactions.

Paper Money in the United States

As early as the 1680s, many American Colonies issued their own paper money. It usually was valued in English pounds, shillings, and pence, or in Spanish reals—or dollars—and their fractions. Printers used the letterpress (with an inked raised surface) and intaglio printing (that used inked engraved plates) to print the notes. In Massachusetts, Paul Revere engraved printing plates for several issues of that colony's notes.

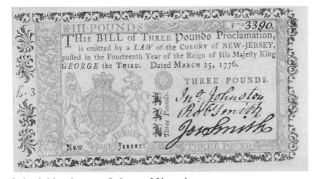

Colonial bank note, Colony of New Jersey

That's Not Worth a Continental!

To finance the American Revolution, the Continental Congress authorized the issue of paper money in the form of certificates. These "Continentals" had no backing in silver or gold, although it was understood that the bearer was entitled to a certain amount of gold or silver. As the war with the British wore on, the Continental Congress continued to print money and caused one of the worst monetary depressions in America's history. People were lucky to redeem the currency for only 2$\frac{1}{2}$ cents on the dollar.

Notes were printed in sheets and then numbered and signed by hand, usually by two, three, and sometimes as many as six people. Several members of the Continental Congress and othres who signed the Declaration of Independence inked their names onto the paper money.

Several Colonies added a second ink color to the type, or a third color to part of the design, to deter counterfeiting. Benjamin Franklin developed a method of using detailed impressions of leaves as a design feature. This technique was used for more than 60 years.

Many of the notes paid interest and could be exchanged, or redeemed, for the value. A large circular hole punched into the note served as a cancellation mark. Various states saved these redeemed notes for years, so collectors can easily acquire them—they are readily available to collectors.

Civil War Paper Money

The federal government issued paper money on a large scale for the first time in 1861. Because enormous sums were needed to finance the Union's fight against the Confederacy, the government printed paper money in denominations from $1 through

Confederate currency, 1864

$1,000. These greenbacks, nicknamed for the green ink on the *back*, were the start of a national paper currency. The Union also issued notes in denominations of 3 cents, 5 cents, 10 cents, 15 cents, 25 cents, and 50 cents. Collectors call these notes Fractional currency because they are fractions of a dollar. The government printed them through 1876.

The Confederacy also issued paper money during this time. Like broken bank notes, early Confederate money was printed on one side only. Later, to stop counterfeiting, notes were printed with designs on both sides. In 1862, the Confederate government issued "bluebacks" that had blue engravings on the back.

Broken Bank Notes

Starting in the 1790s, but mainly after the War of 1812, cities and private banks and companies printed paper currency to promote commerce. These notes were backed by nothing but the success of the issuer. If a particular bank closed, a holder of that bank's notes could not collect any coin currency from the bank. During the financial panic of the late 1830s, many of the issuers went broke. Collectors call the notes of this era "broken bank notes." After 1872 only the federal government could issue legal tender paper currency.

U.S. Federal Paper Currency

From 1861 to 1929, the federal government issued notes sized approximately 7¹/₄ by 3¹/₈ inches. Collectors call them "large size currency." In 1928, the government reduced the size of U.S. paper money to 6 by 2¹/₂ inches. Collectors call these notes "small size currency."

Small Size Currency

Denominations	Face Design	Back Design
$1	George Washington	Ornate (typeface) ONE and U.S. Seal
$2	Thomas Jefferson	Monticello (red seal) 1928–1957
$2	Thomas Jefferson	Declaration of Independence Signing (green seal) 1976–present
$5	Abraham Lincoln	Lincoln Memorial
$10	Alexander Hamilton	U.S. Treasury Building
$20	Andrew Jackson	The White House
$50	Ulysses S. Grant	U.S. Capitol Building
$100	Benjamin Franklin	Independence Hall
$500	William McKinley	Ornate (typeface) FIVE HUNDRED
$1,000	Grover Cleveland	Ornate (typeface) ONE THOUSAND
$5,000	James Madison	Ornate (typeface) FIVE THOUSAND
$10,000	Salmon P. Chase	Ornate (typeface) TEN THOUSAND
$100,000	Woodrow Wilson	Ornate (typeface) ONE HUNDRED THOUSAND

Since the 1934C series, denominations above $100 have not been printed. The $100,000 note was never intended for circulation, but for bank-to-bank transfers of large amounts of money.

Today's paper currency is printed in sheets of 32 subjects, or notes. When notes are damaged in the printing process, the full sheet is replaced with a sheet of notes bearing serial numbers with a star as the suffix. These "star notes" are quite collectible.

By matching the check letter and quadrant number on a note to the chart shown here, you can determine the position of the note on the uncut sheet of 32 subjects.

32-Subject Sheet with Check Letters and Quadrant Numbers

A1	E1	A2	E2
B1	F1	B2	F2
C1	G1	C2	G2
D1	H1	D2	H2
A3	E3	A4	E4
B3	F3	B4	F4
C3	G3	C4	G4
D3	H3	D4	H4

The U.S. Bureau of Engraving and Printing produces all federal paper currency. It has two facilities that print notes. The first is in Washington, D.C., where the bureau headquarters is located. The second is in Fort Worth, Texas (opened in 1991). A note printed in Fort Worth has a small FW near the lower right signature on the *face.*

To prevent counterfeiting, printers used security measures such as fine engraving, unique paper, special inks, and *watermarks.* They later added special serial numbers to the *bank notes.* Currently, paper money includes state-of-the art security features: strips embedded in the notes, holograms, microprinting, and color-shifting ink.

12 Federal Reserve Districts, with Corresponding Numbers and Letters

1	A	Boston, Massachusetts
2	B	New York, New York
3	C	Philadelphia, Pennsylvania
4	D	Cleveland, Ohio
5	E	Richmond, Virginia
6	F	Atlanta, Georgia
7	G	Chicago, Illinois
8	H	St. Louis, Missouri
9	I	Minneapolis, Minnesota
10	J	Kansas City, Kansas
11	K	Dallas, Texas
12	L	San Francisco, California

The Federal Reserve System

The Bureau of Engraving and Printing produces paper currency based on amounts ordered by the Federal Reserve Board. It ships 8 billion notes each year to the 12 Federal Reserve banks and their 25 branch banks. Those 37 banks formally issue coins and notes to commercial banks for the public to use.

The Federal Reserve System divides the country into 12 districts. A number and a letter on the bank note identify the issuing Federal Reserve district.

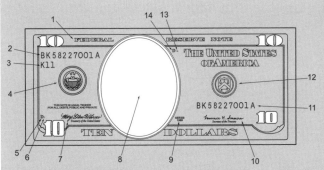

*The diagram of the 10-dollar note illustrates the position of various parts and symbols found on modern U.S. paper currency. The positions of some elements will differ with each denomination.

Anatomy of a Note*

1. **Type of note.** Federal Reserve Note, Silver Certificate, United States Note, National Currency. Gold Certificates do not have the type heading in the usual position at the top.

2. **Serial number.** Every note has two identical serial numbers. The alphabetical suffix (in this case "A") indicates the print run cycle.

3. **Federal Reserve District numbers.** Found only on Federal Reserve Notes.

4. **Federal Reserve Bank seal.** Found only on Federal Reserve Notes.

5. **Check letters.** Each note has two identical check letters which indicate its position on the full printed sheet.

6. **Quadrant number.** The number (from 1 to 4) represents the quadrant on 32-subject sheets.

7. **Signature of the Treasurer of the United States.**

8. **Portrait.** Each denomination carries a distinctive portrait.

9. **Series date.** The indicated position is for notes of later years. Earlier printings carry the series date two times on the face, and in varying positions.

10. **Signature of the Secretary of the Treasury.**

11. See No. 2.

12. **Treasury seal.** The seal may be blue, green, red, brown, gold, or yellow.

13. **Faceplate serial number.** The serial number, consisting of the lower right check letter and the adjacent number, indicates the specific plate from which the note was printed.

14. See No. 5.

Tokens, Medals, and Decorations

Tokens, medals, and decorations serve unique purposes and have a different kind of value from traditional coins.

Tokens

Tokens are substitute coins issued by merchants, city governments, clubs, or individuals that do not normally have the right to mint coins. The public understands their value. A token, usually made of a base metal like tin or brass, is worth less than its stated value. A token might carry a legend that tells how the token can be used, such as for a car wash or video game. But the people distributing and using a token understand what its value is. Apart from its specific use, the token is generally worthless unless it can be exchanged for something else with someone who can use it.

Some tokens do have monetary value and are used like real coins, such as the subway tokens used in New York City. Others, like the casino slot-machine token, are redeemable for cash. A third kind of token, the store card, is good for services or merchandise only.

Two special groups of tokens worth studying and collecting are Hard Times tokens and Civil War tokens. An economic downturn in the 1830s led to a shortage of small change, and copper tokens were manufactured to provide emergency coins.

Don't Take Any Wooden Nickels!

At one time, wooden nickels were used as currency at state fairs. Local town merchants accepted the tokens and gave them back as change because everyone could spend them at the fair. But as the event drew to a close, store-keepers quit taking the wooden nickels because they knew they might not have a chance to cash them in before the fair ended.

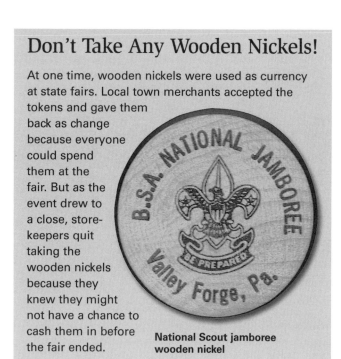

National Scout jamboree wooden nickel

These Hard Times tokens bear politically inspired legends. During the Civil War (1861–1865), people hoarded money because they were worried about the war's outcome. With small change scarce, merchants in the North issued store tokens, and others produced generic tokens with patriotic slogans. Collectors like the merchant tokens for their regional interest and the patriotic tokens for their national appeal.

Medals

Medals have no monetary value in commerce. They are large, usually round metal objects struck as awards, commemorative items, or art pieces. Award metals recognize achievements such as long service, heroic acts, or sports victories. Commemorative medals honor people, events, and places. Art medals are created for aesthetic purposes.

Many medals, such as this Charles Schulz memorial medal, are available from the U.S. Mint. You can request a complete list of medals that are available.

Decorations

Decorations are awards presented to individuals for service to a country or organization, which often includes heroism and participation in military actions. Because they are meant to be worn, decorations come in forms such as badges, stars, and sashes.

Freaks, Fakes, and False Money

A common error happens when a planchet is improperly centered. The collar can't completely surround the blank, so the coin is struck off-center.

Some coins and paper money are altered by mistake; some are altered by intention.

Errors

In coin production, mistakes are called mint *errors*. And they are collectible. Although currency is carefully inspected before it is shipped to the Federal Reserve banks, some errors slip into circulation. Errors fall into three groups.

- Planchet errors occur before the coin is struck. The coin blanks can be damaged, clipped, or broken. A common error is the eclipsed planchet. This happens when a circular piece is cut out of the planchet because the metal strip was misaligned during the blanking process.

- Striking errors occur during the minting of the coin. A "freak" is a major error so strange that people wonder how it could have happened—for example, a coin with two obverses.

- Die errors cause small differences among coins of the same type. These are called die varieties. Dies chip, break, crack, and rotate. Until the die is replaced, it will cause the same change to each coin it strikes. For example, a *die crack* creates a raised line on the struck coin.

Collectors love the *mule,* a blank struck with two dies not meant to be used together. This results in an odd coin, such as a quarter obverse with a dollar reverse, which makes a $1.25 coin!

Common paper errors include slightly off-center notes, white spots on notes where the bill was folded, ink smears, and cutting errors. An inverted error occurs when a sheet is fed upside down in the final stage, so that signatures and serial numbers appear upside down.

Even mint errors must be in perfect condition to get the best price. And beware of fake mistakes!

Radial flow lines on a coin are created when the planchet is struck. The extent to which the lines reflect light is a coin's luster.

The most desirable paper money error is a note with the face of one denomination matched with the back design of another denomination, creating a dual denomination note, such as the face of a $5 bill with the back of a $10 bill.

Altered Coins

Some coins are faked to resemble other, more valuable coins. The alterations are deliberate changes made by someone who wants to profit by making the coins appear rare and desirable.

Common alterations include changing mint marks and dates. For example, the 1914D cent is more valuable than the 1914 cent with no mint mark, so tricky fakers add a D to a 1914 plain cent and try to pass it off as a 1914D.

A buffed coin has been polished to make it look shiny, like an uncirculated or proof coin. Use a magnifying glass to check the amount of wear on the high points of the design. True luster caused from the pressure of striking a coin cannot be duplicated or restored by polishing. Severe polishing with a wire brush or wheel also can alter the surface of a coin.

Collectors consider altered coins to be damaged and, therefore, nearly worthless. If you study a coin series and know what genuine coins look like, you will recognize an altered coin when you see one.

Counterfeits

Counterfeit, or false, money has been around as long as official currency. Two major types of counterfeits are substitute money, which is made to fool merchants, and forgeries, which are made to fool collectors.

Counterfeit coins can be cast or die-struck. Cast counterfeits are more common because it is easier and cheaper to make a casting mold from a real coin than it is to engrave a look-alike die. Counterfeiters often used lead to make copies of silver coins in circulation. As long as the coins were not dropped on a counter, they could pass for silver coins. Struck silver coins have a distinctive "ring" when dropped, which cast lead does not.

Clad coinage has replaced precious metal coins for circulation, and many counterfeiters believe that late 20th-century coins are not worth copying. Because high-value coins no longer circulate, counterfeiters often focus on paper money.

Forgers look for big profits from unwary collectors. They cast bullion coins or invest in expensive equipment to make die-struck counterfeits of rare coins.

Many older reproductions, or copies, were made for collectors so they could show a sample of a scarce design in their collections. These copies often were cast in two-part molds and have a telltale seam on the edge where the two mold halves joined. To distinguish reproductions from counterfeits, the Hobby Protection Act of 1973 requires reproductions to be marked with the word COPY.

How can you tell if a coin is a counterfeit or forgery? Look at coins in books, at coin shows, and in collections. Know what the real coin should look like. A cast counterfeit might be smaller than the real coin, or feel greasy to the touch. The reeding or lettering on the edge might be imperfect. The field might show pitting or bubbles. If you suspect a coin is counterfeit, have an authentication service look at it.

Building Your Own Collection

Collect what pleases you . . . within your budget. You will find out a lot about history and politics by collecting common coins, tokens, or paper money. You can also find out a lot about investing by studying rare coins. And you will certainly find out about economics when you try to buy a coin.

To complete the requirements, you will assemble two different sets of coins. One is a denomination set, with the six different circulating denominations. The other is a *date set* of a single *type*. For that, you will choose one design (type) of a particular denomination and collect a coin from each date for that series, starting with the year of your birth. For example, you might choose the Roosevelt dime or the Jefferson nickel.

For your own collection, you can build a *type set*. Maybe you want to tackle a broad area, such as a 20th-century type set. For that, you would have to collect every design (type) of every denomination issued since 1900. You can narrow your type set to one denomination with all its types within a certain time period.

What Determines Value?

Three factors usually determine the value of a numismatic object:

- Rarity—how many like items exist and are available to acquire
- Condition—the state of preservation
- Demand—how many people want it

A fourth factor is the metal content. This is a coin's intrinsic value. An item that is not rare, in good condition, or in high demand might be expensive just because of the value of the gold or silver metal in it. The metal value establishes a base, or floor value.

Let's say a coin had a mintage in the millions and many examples are still available in the highest condition, but only a hundred people want to buy the coin. Because the supply is high and demand low, it would not cost much to buy the coin, and you would not get much if you sold it.

If only a few coins of a type are available and they are not in good condition, but hundreds of collectors are interested in them, the price will be high. If one of those coins is of the best condition and in high demand, you will see record price levels reached each time it is offered.

As a collector, keep records of all your numismatic purchases and sales. File your receipts. Create an inventory ledger for your collection. Be sure to include the amount paid, the date, the seller or buyer, and a useful description of the item or items. This information will help you track your costs. It might also be required for tax purposes when the value increases and for identification if the collection is lost or stolen.

Uncirculated (UNC)

Extremely Fine (EF)

Very Fine (VF)

Fine (F)

Very Good (VG)

Good (G)

Different grades of the same coin

The Condition of Coins

One of the most important elements in determinig the value of an item is its condition, or how well it has been preserved. The *Official ANA Grading Standards for United States Coins,* from the American Numismatic Association, is the accepted reference on grading and offers complete details and illustrations of coins in each grade.

Since the mid-1980s, some professional authentication and grading services have provided a service of grading a coin and encapsulating it, along with an identification card, within a sealed plastic holder commonly referred to as a *slab.* This practice is intended to reduce disagreements over grade. These services are commonly called third-party grading services, which implies that the service provider does not have an ownership interest in the coin being graded and is likely to give a neutral and fair opinion of the coin's condition.

Uncirculated (UNC). A coin that looks as new as the day it was minted. No evidence of any wear.

Extremely Fine (EF). A coin that has every appearance of being in perfect condition, with the exception of very minor flaws or slight wear on high design points.

Very Fine (VF). A coin that shows signs of having been in circulation, with the highest points on the coin design noticeably flattened from wear. It still has fine details in the remaining portions of the design and no disfiguring nicks or scratches.

Fine (F). A coin worn from considerable use. Many parts of the coin, including the outer raised rim, are rounded or flattened from wear; minor nicks and blemishes are visible. The overall appearance, however, is still pleasing, and all major details show clearly.

Very Good (VG). A coin that shows much wear on the design and surface, although the legends are still readable. The rim is very flat.

Good (G). A coin that is so worn that most of the details are flat.

Poor. A coin that is holed, badly scratched, bent, dented, or worn so much that its type is unidentifiable or barely identifiable.

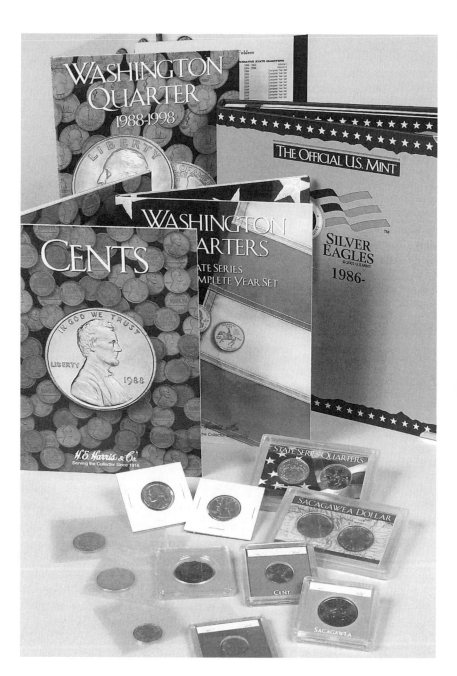

Cleaning, Care, and Storage

Should you clean your coins? Resist the temptation! Never clean proof or uncirculated coins. However, if you want to get some grime off circulated coins, use liquid soap diluted with water. Then pat dry with a soft cloth. Wiping or rubbing a coin will leave surface hairlines that are noticeable under magnification. Cleaning coins with abrasives or silver polish will leave scratches on the surface and chemicals in the recessed areas of the design. Abrasives give the surface an unnatural color and can greatly decrease the numismatic value of the coin.

Cleaning coins using a "dipping" solution will leave the coin with an unnaturally bright appearance. Sometimes these acids etch the surface and damage the coin.

How you store your coins affects their condition and, ultimately, their value. Coins tossed on a table, carried loosely in your pocket, or jumbled together in a felt bag will pick up scratches and nicks. Always hold a coin by the rim, never by the coin's flat faces where fingerprints can easily damage the surfaces. Over time, oils from the skin will react with the metal.

Choose a way to store your coins based on the condition and value of your collection: The better the condition of your coins, the more specialized the protection should be. Some collectors house their coins in slabs and store them in safe-deposit boxes. Do not use products (such as plastic sandwich bags, plastic envelopes, or brown paper envelopes) that contain sulfur, acids, foam rubber, oily substances, and polyvinyl chloride (PVC); they will ruin your coins. Mylar® is a commonly used safe and clear material.

Be sure to keep valuable coins and paper money in a safe and secure place, away from moisture and out of direct sunlight.

Pressed-cardboard coin albums, the most popular storage holders, allow coins to be viewed from one or both sides. They are appropriate for inexpensive coins.

These white cardboard 2-by-2-inch holders have clear film-covered slots the size of common circulating coins. A coin is placed inside the holder, then the cardboard is folded over and stapled to hold the coin in place. Descriptive information can be recorded on the holder. These holders can be stored in made-to-fit boxes.

Plastic 2-by-2-inch holders, often called "flips," have one pouch to hold the coin and another to hold identification. Close the holder by flipping, or folding, it over.

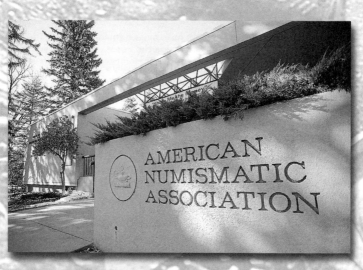

Museum at the headquarters of the American Numismatic
Association in Colorado Springs, Colorado

Great Coin Collections on Display

As you learn more about numismatics, you might want to see some of the great coins of the world for yourself. Or maybe you have realized that you have a special interest in a particular part of the coin collecting hobby. As you put your own collection together, you will enjoy discovering how great collections have been assembled.

The American Numismatic Association, the largest organization in the world for coin collectors, houses a public display of coins, medals, and paper money in its museum in Colorado Springs, Colorado.

The American Numismatic Society, located in New York City, has a permanent collection called the World of Coins, which traces the history of coins from ancient times to the present.

The National Numismatic Collection at the Smithsonian Institution in Washington, D.C., is featured in a special exhibition area in the Museum of American History. The archives of the Bureau of Engraving and Printing are housed at the Smithsonian.

Specialty organizations have their own collections of transit tokens, modern art medals, copper coins of the Colonial era, paper money, and patterns. For example, check out the Wooden Nickel Historical Museum in San Antonio, Texas. You should be able to find a collection of whatever interests you. If not, start your own!

Coin Collecting Resources

Scouting Literature

Collections and *Stamp Collecting* merit badge pamphlets

Books

Breen, Walter H. *Walter Breen's Complete Encyclopedia of U.S. and Colonial Coins.* Doubleday, 1988.

Bressett, Ken, and Abe Kasoff, eds. and comps. *The Official A.N.A. Grading Standards for United States Coins.* 5th ed. St. Martin's Press, 1996.

Edler, Joel T., and David C. Harper, eds. *U.S. Coin Digest: A Guide to Average Retail Prices from the Market Experts.* Krause Publications, 2004.

Harper, David C., ed. *2003 North American Coins and Prices: A Guide to U.S., Canadian and Mexican Coins.* 12th ed. Krause Publications, 2002.

Krause, Chester L., Robert F. Lemke, and Joel T. Edler, eds. *Standard Catalog of U.S. Paper Money.* 22nd rev. ed. Krause Publications, 2003.

Krause, Chester L., and Clifford Mishler. *2004 Standard Catalog of World Coins: 1901–Present.* 32nd ed. Krause Publications, 2004.

———. *Standard Catalog of World Coins: 1801–1900.* 4th ed. Krause Publications, 2004.

———. *Standard Catalog of World Coins: 1701–1800.* 3rd ed. Krause Publications, 2002.

———. *Standard Catalog of World Coins: 1601–1700.* 3rd ed. Krause Publications, 2003.

Ruddy, James F. *Photograde: A Photographic Grading Encyclopedia for United States Coins.* 18th ed. St. Martin's Press, 1996.

Shafer, Neil, and Colin R. Bruce II, eds. *Standard Catalog of World Paper Money: General Issues 1365–1960.* 9th ed. Krause Publications, 2000.

Shafer, Neil, and George S. Cuhaj, eds. *Standard Catalog of World Paper Money: Modern Issues 1961–2003.* 9th ed. Krause Publications, 2003.

Slabaugh, Arlie R. *Confederate States Paper Money.* Krause Publications, 2001.

Yeoman, R. S. *A Guide Book of United States Coins.* 59th edition. St. Martin's Press, 2004.

Magazines

COINage (monthly)
Miller Magazines Inc.
4880 Market St.
Ventura, CA 93003
Web site: *http://www.coinagemag.com*

Coin Prices (bimonthly)
Krause Publications Inc.
700 E. State St.
Iola, WI 54990
Web site:
http://www.coinpricesmagazine.net

Coins Magazine (monthly)
Krause Publications Inc.
700 E. State St.
Iola, WI 54990
Web site: *http://www.coinsmagazine.net*

The Numismatist (monthly)
American Numismatic Association
818 N. Cascade Ave.
Colorado Springs, CO 80903
Web site: *http://www.money.org/
publicationsdept.html*

Newspapers

Bank Note Reporter (monthly)
Krause Publications
700 E. State St.
Iola, WI 54990
Web site:
http://www.banknotereporter.com

Coin World (weekly)
Amos Press Inc.
P.O. Box 150
Sidney, OH 45365
Web site: *http://www.coinworld.com*

Numismatic News (weekly)
Krause Publications Inc.
700 E. State St.
Iola, WI 54990
Web site:
http://www.numismaticnews.net

World Coin News (monthly)
Krause Publications, Inc.
700 East State Street
Iola, WI 54990
Web site: *http://www.worldcoinnews.net*

Organizations and Numismatic Web Sites

American Medallic Sculpture Association
P.O. Box 1201
Edmonds, WA 98020
Web site: *http://www.amsamedals.org/*

American Numismatic Association
818 N. Cascade Ave.
Colorado Springs, CO 80903
Web site: *http://www.money.org*

American Numismatic Club Listings
Web site: *http://www.money.org/
clublist.html*

American Numismatic Society
Broadway at 155th Street
New York, NY 10032
Web site: *http://amnumsoc.org*

Civil War Token Society
26548 Mazur Drive
Rancho Palos Verdes, CA 90275
Web site: *http://www.cwtsociety.com*

CoinFacts.com
Web site: *http://www.coinfacts.com*

CoinLink
Web site: *http://www.coinlink.com*

Federal Reserve Districts

Web site: *http://www.
federalreserve.gov/otherfrb.htm*

National Numismatic Collection

National Museum of American History
Smithsonian Institution
14th Street and Constitution Avenue, NW
Washington, DC 20560
Web site: *http://americanhistory.
si.edu/csr/cadnnc.htm*

Society of Paper Money Collectors

P.O. Box 117060
Carrollton, TX 75011
Web site: *http:www.spmc.org*

Society of U.S. Pattern Collectors

Web site: *http://www.uspatterns.com*

United States Bureau of Engraving and Printing

14th and C Streets, SW
Washington, DC 20228
Web site: *http://www.moneyfactory.com*

United States Mint

Customer Care Center
801 9th St., NW
Washington, DC 20220
Web site: *http://www.usmint.gov*

Acknowledgments

The Boy Scouts of America gives
bountiful thanks to George Cuhaj
of the editorial staff of the *Standard
Catalog of World Coins* for his
guidance, assistance, and dedication
throughout the development of this
new edition of the *Coin Collecting* merit
badge pamphlet. Mr. Cuhaj serves as
chair of the American Numismatic
Association's Boy Scout Merit Badge
Committee, and has organized the
ANA's participation in every Merit
Badge Midway of the BSA's national
Scout jamboree since 1981. He has been
actively associated with the American
Numismatic Society and Stack's Rare
Coins (New York) for many years and
currently serves on Krause Publication's
editorial and *Standard Catalog of World
Coins* staffs.

Thanks also to staff members at
the American Numismatic Society,
the American Numismatic Association,
Stack's Rare Coins, and Krause
Publications, and to individuals David
C. Kranz, Thomas Michael, Lee Hartz,
and Tom Casper for their contributions
to this pamphlet.

Photo credits

George Cuhaj, courtesy—page 12 *(center)*

Dynamic Graphics Inc., ©Clipper May
1998—pages 8 and 12 *(background)*

Dynamic Graphics Inc., ©Clipper August
2001—page 20 *(both)*

©Image Source/elektraVision/
PictureQuest—page 16

Krause Publications, Iola, Wisconsin,
and Stack's Rare Coins, New York,
New York, courtesy—pages 13, 18
(all), 21 *(both)*, 22 *(all)*, 23 *(all)*,
25 *(both)*, 26 *(both)*, 27 *(top six)*,
28 *(both)*, 29 *(all)*, 30 *(both)*, 31
(all), 35, 36, 37, 45 *(top two)*, 46,
47, and 54 *(all)*

The following photos and all others
not mentioned above are the property
of or are protected by the Boy Scouts
of America.

Brian Payne—page 60

Randy Piland—cover, pages 6, 32, 52,
and 57